- Successful Dating -

No More Frogs
Aquarius

20 January – 18 February

by
Cathrine Dahl

CONTENTS

- Successful Dating -
No More Frogs

by Cathrine Dahl

No More Frogs - Successful Dating is your one-stop dating guide. No unnecessary blah-blah. The information is right here, at your fingertips.

This guide can be used in many different ways. It's a handy tool when you want to prepare yourself a little before going on a blind date, or getting to know someone you've just met - or even someone you've known for a while.

Although this guide can help you angle your approach, remember to be true to yourself. Have fun, be wise, follow your heart - and keep your feet on the ground!

- Cathrine Dahl

Preface:
A few words about compatibility, and why compatibility guides suck.

So you've met this Gemini you really, really like, but you're a Scorpio, and the compatibility guides say you're a lousy match. Guess what? That's rubbish!

Many compatibility guides offer a very simplistic approach, claiming that your best matches are the star signs that share the same element as you:

Fire: Aries, Leo and Sagittarius
Earth: Taurus, Virgo and Capricorn
Air: Gemini, Libra and Aquarius
Water: Cancer, Scorpio and Pisces

Other guides are slightly less specific, declaring that we are only compatible with star signs within our own astrological polarity.

Yin: Taurus, Virgo, Capricorn, Cancer, Scorpio and Pisces
Yang: Aries, Leo, Sagittarius, Gemini, Libra and Aquarius

Doesn't look too good, does it? Even the more optimistic approach has removed half of the population from your dating pool. Of course, this doesn't make any sense. Reality is far more promising.

One star sign, two very different personalities

Each of us has a unique astrological thumb print. This is determined by the ten planets and twelve astrological houses. The most important factors are your ascending star (ascendant), your sun star (star sign) and your moon (which governs your feelings).

Let's make it simple

Imagine your star sign as a melody. All the other aspects (the unique positioning of the planets and houses) are sound effects applied by a DJ or a producer.

The combination of rhythm, depth and base creates your unique sound. Another person with the same star sign/melody will have his own mix and end up with a different beat.

Your individual sound can create wonderful harmonies with star signs you're not supposed to get on with - and nothing but noise with signs that are meant to be matches. You won't find out until you get to know each other.

Let's get to know your date...

THE MALE

YOUR DATE: AQUARIUS
20 January – 18 February

The Essence of him

A true individualist – spontaneous – colourful – checks out new things – shows genuine interest – loves to figure things out – intrigued by the human mind – no problem acquiring wisdom and knowledge from others – not impressed by titles or money – seeks truth and knowledge – strong intuition – emotionally detached – loves to stand out – self-disciplined – does not conform

...and remember: He won't enter into close friendships before he is certain about people's intentions. Earning his trust takes time.

Blind Date – speedy essentials

Who's waiting for you?

No one, because he will probably be late. He has 1000 things going in his mind and is easily distracted when something captures his interest. After having waited ten minutes or so, keep an eye out for a guy who sticks out in one way or another – maybe a slightly unusual hairstyle or piece of clothing. He will approach you as a friend and start talking about something interesting he's been thinking about. Remember, you are on a date with the individualist of the zodiac. Anything can happen. Prepare yourself for all sorts of spontaneous and weird conversations.

Emergency fixes for embarrassing pauses

If he likes you, he will always come up with something to talk about – even though it may not interest you all that much. His social antenna can be a little off-base at times. Should he run out of topics, which is very unlikely, go ahead and fill in. Talk about anything from music to the occult, but make sure to show some depth. This man can't stand superficial people.

Your place or mine?

Sex on the first date? No problem. If you hit it off, he won't mind joining you back at home to share a bottle wine or a some exotic snacks. He is very much an adventurer. A new partner represents new turf for him to explore. He is not a naturally passionate guy, and the erotic feelings will take time to develop – provided he feels inspired. You may end up spending the night talking instead.

Checklist, before you dash out to meet him:

Bring a small, unusual gift or surprise
(hint: Make it very special)
Wear a piece of jewelery that stands out
(hint: Make him curious)
Check out new restaurants ahead of time
(hint: He'd love something new)
Have some interesting knowledge ready to share
(hint: He loves to explore and learn)
Be prepared to raise a few erotic ideas
(hint: Make it exotic, but not crude)

Tip: He will welcome anything that can broaden his horizon, especially if it's a little out of the ordinary. This applies to his sex life as well – but avoid anything vulgar.

CHAPTER 1

PREPARE YOURSELF

**Catch his eye, capture his attention
Top 10 attention grabbers**

1. Take the initiative, but be subtle.
2. Tell him about exotic places you've visited, or want to visit, and why.
3. Make sure there's something unusual about you (hair, clothing, jewelery, etc).
4. Don't reveal too much. Keep a slight aura of mystery.
5. Inspire him. He loves learning new things.
6. Don't be aggressive. Make him feel relaxed in your company.
7. Be feminine, soft and a little innocent in your demeanour.
8. Let there be something unique about you, something that makes you stand out.
9. Present him with an interesting challenge that needs to be solved.
10. Listen and ask smart questions.

The SHE. The woman!

Some may claim that this man's dream woman is almost a fantasy. His expectations are many and specific. Feminine charm is not enough: she must also be alert and intelligent, sparking his interest and making him curious about her and life in general. She needs to be soft and feminine, as well as independent and strong. His ideal woman is a free spirit who allows him to take the lead. Most importantly, she must also be his friend and companion – and an adventurous lover.

The Essence of her

Alert – flexible – independent – feminine and sweet – supportive and interested in his ideas and projects – a constant challenge and a source of inspiration – interesting, with an appetite for the mysteries of life – a free spirit – adventurous – liberated – optimistic – slightly mysterious – erotically exciting – open-minded – open to topics that are a little out of the ordinary

Aquarius' arousal meter

From 0 to 100... in an hour - or several days. It depends on whether it's a dawning mystery or sudden adventure.

Remember: Be true to yourself

It doesn't matter if he is the most stunning guy you've ever met – if you don't match, you don't match. You may be able to put on a show for a while to hold his attention, but what's the point? We can't please everybody. We all have different needs, dreams, tastes and preferences. There's no such thing as a one-size-fits-all lover. Be yourself, and be true to who you are – always!

Very important: Don't rush him, either in sex or romance. He needs to get to know you and feel comfortable around you, before he makes up his mind.

CHAPTER 2

THE FIRST DATE

Getting your foot in the door
The basics

Trigger his mind. Forget about dressing up in a sexy outfit. He will either look at you strangely or not notice at all. You need to appeal to his mind, not his toolbox.

Inspire him. If you manage to introduce him to new topics, people and exciting places, you'll have his attention.

Make a move. He can be quite shy, which is why he prefers a woman to make the first move. This doesn't mean you can run him over like a steamroller. Guide him gently.

Give him space. If you try to dominate him or boss him around, he'll be off.

Free your spirit. If you're really serious about him, let him know that you appreciate freedom as much as he does.

In the mood? Be smart about it. This guy isn't easily seduced. He needs to appreciate you as a person before he will become erotically involved. If you are in a hurry, tell him you need someone to teach you a thing or two. This could work - or it could result in a lecture on lovemaking.

Whatever you do...

• DON'T come across as aggressive or too assertive.

• DON'T be argumentative and fixed in your opinions.

• DON'T criticise others for being original.

• DON'T wear overly suggestive clothing.

• DON'T push him into making a decision.

Remember,
don't reveal too much right away. Keep him guessing. He loves the suspense.

- **DON'T make fun of his unusual ideas.**

- **DON'T ask him what kind of salary he's aiming for.**

- **DON'T keep looking at your watch, telling him that sleep is a priority.**

- **DON'T refuse to see things from new perspectives.**

- **DON'T get distracted from what he's saying.**

There must be loads of room for mysteries for him to figure out. Never allow him to read you like an open book.

Signs you're in - or not

Keep in mind that a relationship with him will usually start as a friendship, and that every friendship takes a while for him to establish. However, on a rare occasion, a mysterious and interesting woman may ignite his romantic dreams and drive him to pursue her without the usual get-to-know-each-other-first phase. In that case, she'll need to live up to the vision he has created of her. Could be fun. Could be a challenge. Could be absolutely worth it! If you have managed to turn him into a romantic explorer, you will probably start to notice a thing or two...

Chances are he will...

- invite you out for an unusual meal or a drink
- suggest listening to some new music while taking a herbal bath
- keep you up late at night to explore books or movies
- change or adjust his style in order to impress you
- serve you exotic fruits or drinks
- be willing to explore erotic mysteries with you

Not your type? Making an exit

An Aquarius man will never let anything or anyone hold him back or restrict his freedom. If things are not working out, he will be off before you've even had a chance to think about it. There will be no drama – just an exit. It takes a very special woman to compel him to commit to a long-term relationship. Either it feels right, or it doesn't. He's basically looking to date a soul-mate. A fling might be fun, but it will take more than an interesting erotic adventure to keep him around.

However, if you are the one who's had enough, and he doesn't get it, he's probably far too absorbed in a project or busy turning you into a dream woman in his mind. No need to worry. Getting an Aquarius to pack his bags is easy. If you have reached this stage, you need to get his attention.

Foolproof exit measures:

There's no need to go over the top. Simple things and suggestions can make this man freak out. Here are a few examples:

- Get jealous and ask him where he has been and with whom
- Make a fuss about his mess and tell him to be tidier
- Insist on talking about feelings and make him commit to the future
- Become rigid and conservative in your views
- Get angry and upset whenever he's late - for anything
- Introduce routines to 'help him' become more efficient

CHAPTER 3

SEX'N STUFF

Seductive moves:
How to get him in the mood:

The Aquarius's mind is probably his biggest erogenous zone. You won't get far without appealing to his thoughts and fantasies. You need to present your ideas as suggestions. Allow him to visualize the possibilities and let them sink in. Make the surroundings comfortable and a little exotic. Pillows are great, and they can be handy during the erotic adventure...

Preferences and erotic nature

He is willing to try most things - once. His constant need for change applies to his sex life as well. He wants sex at different times, day and night. As far as positions are concerned, he is probably the only male in the zodiac that is capable of making the old missionary position a new adventure every time you try it. He is playful, but he seldom wastes his money on expensive sexual gadgets. He prefers to use his imagination. If he ever uses anything besides his hands and body, it's usually something natural, like oils, creams and chocolate.

Hitting the right buttons

Although every sign has areas on the body that are more sensitive than others, individual sensitivity may vary quite a bit. Don't go body-blind. Honing in on these erogenous zones and forgetting the rest of him is not a good idea. Use these areas to create sparks while turning him on, and as a passion-booster when things get heated. Watch his body language – including the most obvious of signs. Open your mind to the sensuality of touch and taste.

Key areas
Lower legs and ankles

Get it on

If you want spark his erotic interest, pay close attention to his ankles. This area works like an 'on' button, no matter whether you're at home or out in public. Playing footsie in a restaurant can take on a completely new meaning with this man. Kick off your shoes and make sure your feet are nice and soft. The fact that he's being aroused in a public place will add to the excitement.

Arouse him

If he doesn't seem all that keen on sex, it might be a good idea to give him a gentle massage, paying special attention to his feet, calves and ankles. This is usually all it takes to stir up the erotic feelings within him. Make sure to touch him gently. Being too rough will turn him off.

Surprise him

The prospect of experiencing something new is a great turn-on for an Aquarius. Tell him you're studying tantric sex (or something similar) and need someone to practice on. Give him a few hints as to what he may expect...

Spice it up

Tell him about your erotic fantasies – but only the ones you want to try out. Bring a fun erotic toy to bed and allow him to explore you.

Remember: His sex life is ruled by his mind. Sassy underwear alone won't do it. He needs something that triggers his imagination, something inspiring, tantalizing and a little mysterious...

His expectations

Prepare to say yes. He needs a partner with an open mind. More traditional women who prefer it once a week under the covers with the lights out are not his preference.

Go exploring. You don't have to be particularly experienced or creative, provided that you're eager to explore erotic pleasures.

A little creativity makes all the difference. Traditional positions are fine. He will simply try things from a new angle in order to make the sensation more exciting.

Liberate yourself. He expects to expand his sensual horizons by trying new things. Doing the same over and over again will cause him to lose interest.

Take it slow and enjoy the scenery. He loves the erotic journey and can actually be a little indifferent about climaxing – or he may turn it around completely and focus on different ways of experiencing orgasm. He can be a little either/or.

Be ready. He can come up with erotic invitations at the weirdest moments, and he will expect his partner to play along. This can either be very exiting or quite tiring, depending on your preferences.

Your sensual preferences
Quiz yourself and find out whether this man is for you.

Where on the scale are you?
1 = Don't agree | 3 = Sure | 5 = Agree!

1. Orgasm is just a bonus. The erotic journey is far more important.
One a scale for 1 to 5, you are: 1 - 2 - 3- 4 - 5

2. Exploring each other's bodies can be very satisfying.
One a scale for 1 to 5, you are: 1 - 2 - 3- 4 - 5

3. Intense passion can ruin the mysteries of sex.
One a scale for 1 to 5, you are: 1 - 2 - 3- 4 - 5

4. Sex should not be confined to certain times or places.
One a scale for 1 to 5, you are: 1 - 2 - 3- 4 - 5

Score 15–20: You truly enjoy the exotic pleasures of sex and share his need for adventure.
Score 10–14: The relationship will never be boring, and he will probably bring out your adventurous side.
Score 5–9: He wants sex to be fun, exciting and interesting; you appreciate passion and a wonderful finish. You may want to talk things over with him...
Score 1–4: The two of you are not on the same level. Looking for passion, tenderness and closeness? This is not your man.

CHAPTER 4

GENERAL STUFF

The big picture

Keep in mind that the characteristics of an Aquarius may vary quite a bit depending on where within the sign he was born, as well as a wide range of additional astrological factors. But for now, let's stick to the basics. Just remember: don't jump to conclusions as soon as you meet him. Give him room to shine. Get to know the man behind the sign.

His personality: Pros and cons

Pros	Cons
• Open to learn from others	• Restless
• Genuine	• Distracted
• Curious	• Self-obsessed
• Good listener	• Emotionally detached
• Individualist	• Superficial
• Eloquent and convincing	• Drifting
• Very intuitive	• Controlling
• Intelligent	• Distrusting
• Analytical	• A lone wolf
• Self-disciplined	• Prone to withdrawal
• Unconventional	• Indecisive
• Unafraid	• Stubborn
• Explores and moves forward	• Obsessed with freedom
• Creates his own destiny	• Intellectually snobbish

Tip: How to show romantic interest

Be supportive of his ideas. Spend time exploring his interests, and give him a special gift that shows you're paying attention and that you understand him.

Romantic Vibes

Mr Aquarius:
The independent and considerate partner

The essence

Keeping his distance... for a little while. It can be difficult to get to know him. Although he's generous and friendly, he might seem to be holding something back. This is simply because he is afraid to get too close too soon.

Love rocks, but friendship rules. Don't try pushing him into a relationship. Love usually starts with friendship. Sometimes it may seem as though he's more interested in a friend than a girlfriend – but that's just his way.

A playful soul mate. He seeks a partner who is a companion in every area of life.

Commitment and higher love. Romance is important to him, but on a different level – almost intellectual and something to explore and strive towards. When he does get romantically involved, he will devote loads of time to his partner.

Space and room to breathe. He needs freedom to make up his own mind. This is very important for the relationship to work.

No fussing, please! He doesn't like to be told when to go out, where or with whom. This will make him feel trapped and restless.

Tip: How to show erotic interest

Casually guide the conversation in an erotic direction. Ask him for his opinion and let him know that you are curious about whether something is as amazing as it seems to be...

Erotic Vibrations

Mr Aquarius:
The curious and exploring lover

The essence

A slightly unusual lover. Just when you think things are about to get a little steamy, he may start thinking about something unrelated. Suddenly the two of you may find yourselves sitting naked in bed having a lively discussion.

Seizing the erotic moment. He can be so absorbed in foreplay that he forgets about having an orgasm. To him, sex is an adventurous trip into the unknown, and sometimes the trip itself becomes more fascinating than the climax.

From dream to reality. He is not a selfish lover – far from it. He's willing to explore your fantasies and make you experience the pleasure of your erotic dreams.

Loves a challenge. He is a master when it comes to pleasing his partner. If you regard yourself as reserved, with him, you won't remain shy for long! An Aquarius man loves a challenge. Even if he can't arouse you physically, he will probably manage to do so mentally.

Spicy suggestions. Don't expect him to stick to old routines. He needs constant change and new inputs. He may suggest having sex in unusual places and in different ways – anything that may bring excitement into his sex life.

CHAPTER 5

COMPATIBILITY QUIZ

Are you banging your head against the wall, or does he unleash your positive potential? Do you provoke him or bring out the best in him? Does he make you throw your arms up in exasperation, or do you feel inspired and complete in his company? Are the two of you headed towards doom or dream? Take the test to find out.

Question 1
You wake up one morning 'in the mood'. How do you react when your partner ignores all the hints and starts talking about his plans for the day?

A. It's typical. Sometimes I wonder if he fancies me at all.
B. I would be a little upset...
C. That's just who he is. Besides, I know he will make up for it later in the day.

Question 2
Do you mind a man who sometimes gets completely absorbed in himself and his own interests?

A. Not at all. I enjoy guys who get into things.
B. Yes. I can't stand selfish dudes.
C. I don't mind – provided it's not all the time.

(cont.)

Question 3.
Do you think it's possible to get so into foreplay that you forget about an orgasm?

A. I'd like to meet a guy who's that good.
B. Yes, absolutely. Sex is more than steamy passion. It's about playfulness and exploring new sensations.
C. Absolutely not!

Question 4.
Is financial security important to you?

A. Sure, but I'm not hooked on it. As long as I'm happy with my man, I don't mind taking things as they come.
B. Financial insecurity freaks me out.
C. I'm not that good with savings, but I usually have my bills and expenses under control.

Question 5.
Do you mind telling your partner about previous sexual experiences?

A. Not at all. It could be an inspiration for both of us.
B. No, but only if he asks me.
C. Yes – that's too intimate. I like to keep certain things to myself.

Question 6.
Are you a social butterfly, or do you prefer to spend quality time with a few close friends?

A. Having people around me all the time drains me.
B. I'm very social. I love meeting new people.
C. A little bit of both, really. Depends on my mood.

Question 7.
Think about it: Why do you really want a partner?

A. I like having someone to snuggle with.
B. It's nice to have someone to share intimate things with.
C. To experience the unique combination of friendship and sensuality, and have someone bringing out the best in me.

Question 8.
What traits do you usually emphasise when trying to attract a man?

A. My personality and my feminine sides.
B. My body. I have good curves, so why not show them off?
C. My hobbies and interests. There's no point spending a lot of time getting to know a man if we don't have anything in common.

Question 9.
Do you think it's important to be mentally aroused in order to fully enjoy your partner?

A. One usually follows the other. Physical connection leads to mental connection, and the other way around.
B. Is it even possible to have sex without being mentally aroused...?
C. No. That sounds a little weird. As long as my body works, I'm good.

Question 10.
Do you think it's important to explore your erotic life?

A. Yes, I love exploring the mysteries of sex.
B. Sure, it's always fun add a bit of spice.
C. No. Sex is about intimacy and closeness – it's not a creativity contest.

SCORE	A	B	C
Question 1	1	5	10
Question 2	10	1	5
Question 3	5	10	1
Question 4	10	1	5
Question 5	10	5	1
Question 6	1	10	5
Question 7	1	5	10
Question 8	5	1	10
Question 9	5	10	1
Question 10	5	1	10

75 – 100

Wow. This is so good you might be tempted to start believing in fate. The two of you have probably discussed fate already ... or something similar. This relationship will never get boring. You will always be exploring something, inspiring each other and helping each other grow. You share the belief that love happens on a higher level, and the same applies to sex. You complement each other perfectly and love each other's company. The two of you could thrive on a deserted island. Enjoy!

51 – 74

He has entered your life and made everything come alive. Sure, he can be extremely messy and distracted, but there's something about him that helps your overlook the things that would drive other people nuts. If you want to keep him to yourself, you really have to make an effort. This guy is constantly on the move, either in the real world or in his mind. He's not really into romantic evenings – unless there's something new he wants to try; exotic candles, erotic massage or new techniques or flavours. Be flexible and tolerant, and he will bring adventures to your life.

26 – 50

Of course it can be fun to date a man who is completely different to the other guys you've met. He may impress you with knowledge and new ideas, and approach traditional topics from a new angle and turn the day upside down ... but is there something missing? Do you wish you had a little more influence on the relationship? Do you get upset when he loses track of time and shows up two hours late for a date? Are you missing more tenderness and romance in your life? Chances are very slim that Mr Aquarius will change. He may try to please you for a while, but then he'll forget. It might be time to cut through. Give it a shot, but be honest with yourself.

10 – 25

This could be a fun friendship, but hardly a happy and romantic relationship. When it comes to intimacy, you disagree about most things. You set your standards, while he shrugs his shoulders. You voice your opinions, but he starts talking about an interesting album he just listened to. You can criticize as much as you like, or even show your feelings and let him know when you are hurt, but it doesn't really seem to think in. It's almost as if you are talking past each other. Yes, he may be a fun adventure, but it's time for you to start exploring happiness elsewhere.

Thoughts...
Flexibility can turn things around. Communication can open doors. A different approach to an old topic can make you see your partner in a new and colourful light.

THE FEMALE

YOUR DATE: AQUARIUS
20 January – 18 February

The Essence of her

Sensitive – intellectual – impulsive and does things on the spur of the moment – enjoys new activities – loves broadening her horizons – charming – imaginative – stubborn – choosy and waits a long time before entering into a relationship – independent – doesn't mind pursuing hobbies on her own – original – creative – entertaining – manages to discover the positive side of most people – loves having people around

...and remember: She finds men fascinating and usually has quite a few male friends. However, if you have sparked her romantic interest, there's no need to be jealous.

Blind Date – speedy essentials

Who's waiting for you?

The Aquarius woman finds people stimulating and loves places where she can interact with others. She has probably suggested meeting in a lively bar or café. If you're late, or she is early, she will probably already be chatting away with somebody. Remember that for her, a blind date is a chance to get to know someone new. Romance and sensual feelings will come later. She is sparkling and charming, with an alert mind. Men who are looking for a quick catch will be disappointed. She is not into fast fun – unless you actually mean fast fun, like catching a plane somewhere or just doing something out of the ordinary.

Emergency fixes for embarrassing pauses.

Although she can be a little shy, especially if she likes you, there won't be any embarrassing pauses. She has a lot of things to talk about. As soon as you start interacting with her, you'll find her rattling on for hours. If the conversation does become slow and difficult, it probably means you don't have much in common. If this happens, there's no point in dragging it out.

Your place or mine?

Neither. You can use all of your favourite tricks – be funny, interesting and tell her about your amazing massages – but it will get you nowhere. She is neither cold nor difficult to arouse; she simply prefers to wait for that special guy comes around. That doesn't mean she won't hang around with you until the early hours of the morning. If she finds you interesting, she probably will. But don't confuse this with erotic intent.

Checklist, before you dash out to meet her:
Wear something unique (t-shirt, socks)
(hint: Stand out without looking silly)
Have suggestions for what to eat and where to go
(hint: Be creative)
Carry a book or an unusual bag
(hint: A good conversation starter)
Bring a small surprise
(hint: Make it special)
Brush up on an interesting topic
(hint: Be interesting)

Tip: Make sure to set yourself apart with something unusual. Draw her attention with something you wear, something you know or a story about something you've done.

CHAPTER 1

PREPARE YOURSELF

Catch her eye, capture her attention
Top 10 attention grabbers

1. Pay her a compliment for something that others wouldn't have noticed.
2. Show compassion for others and offer your assistance.
3. Don't be afraid to speak out and voice your opinion.
4. Be original and stand out from the crowd.
5. Show creativity, enthusiasm and a positive attitude.
6. Be genuinely interested in her.
7. Introduce her to something new, whether a topic, an exotic spa or an exhibition.
8. Make sure that something about your appearance captures her attention.
9. Suggest trying or making some exotic food.
10. Tell her about something that's on your mind and ask for her opinion.

The HE. The man!

He must be able to appeal to her on many different levels. There must be something special about him – nothing major, just something that makes him stand out from the crowd. The Aquarius woman's perfect partner is an adventurer who can join her in making the days come alive with excitement. He must be independent, but still loyal and trustworthy. He must be a free spirit, but never give her any reason to be jealous. He will be entertaining, inspiring, strong and sensual. And finding him...? No wonder there are so many single Aquarian women.

The Essence of him

Individualistic – creative – adventurous – artistic – entertaining and able to broaden her horizons – a free spirit, but faithful – outgoing – positive and enthusiastic with a fondness for new ideas – independent and confident – open-minded – an erotic explorer who loves sensuality – intelligent with the ability of thinking in new directions – forthcoming and friendly

Aquarius arousal meter
From 0 to 100... Two hours or more. She enjoys exploring sex gradually. She can be spontaneous, but she still takes her time.

Remember: Be true to yourself

It doesn't matter if she is the most stunning girl you've ever met – if you don't match, you don't match. You may be able to put on a show for a while to hold her attention, but what's the point? We can't please everybody. We all have different needs, dreams, tastes and preferences. There's no such thing as a one-size-fits-all lover. Be yourself, and be true to who you are – always!

Very important: You need to appeal to her mind. Be yourself. If you have an original streak, let it show. If you have sparked her mind, her body and heart will follow.

CHAPTER 2

THE FIRST DATE

Getting your foot in the door
The basics

Make the first move. Although sparkling and outgoing, the Aquarius woman may be shy about asking a man out on a date – especially if she really likes him.

Make it special. Take her to a special place. This could be a theatre showing an interesting play or a restaurant that specializes in exotic food.

Be personal. Be smart. Be patient. Make sure she gets a glimpse of your private personality. Show her that you are well read, intelligent and take an interest in current affairs.

Entertain and fascinate. Interesting topics will make her pay attention. She expects her date to entertain her and broaden her horizons.

A creative gift. She loves receiving gifts, especially if they are a little out of the ordinary, but not necessarily expensive.

No verbal erotics. Don't start talking about sex right away – unless it's a fascinating topic you'd like to discuss in a conversational way.

Whatever you do...

- **DON'T** be blunt and limit the conversation to sports etc.

- **DON'T** imply that a woman's place is by a man's side.

- **DON'T** be pushy. Ask to see her again, but do it casually.

- **DON'T** emphasize all the things you don't like.

- **DON'T** scan the menu for the cheapest items.

Remember,
Although she is adventurous and independent, she does need balance and trust in

- **DON'T** suggest getting intimate before you are

comfortable in each other's company.

- **DON'T** get jealous when she bumps into male friends.

- **DON'T** criticize open-minded people with different views.

- **DON'T** provoke her and get into political discussions.

- **DON'T** act macho.

her life. Never make her feel insecure by flirting with other women.

Signs you're in - or not

This is not easy to figure out. An Aquarius woman gets on with men in general and has a comfortable relationship with many of her friends. She can get really shy if she likes a guy, and this doesn't make it any easier. Don't expect her to be direct about it. She is not assertive, even when she is romantically interested. You'll need to look out for subtle hints. She will loosen up after you have taken the initiative, but when is a good time to take the initiative? There are signs that you may have triggered her interest:

Chances are she will...

- spend more time with you than other friends
- open up, talk about herself and risk being vulnerable
- treat you to something special, like a home-cooked meal
- casually touch you and be close to you
- introduce you to her friends
- call and text you frequently – provided you already took the initiative

Not your type? Making an exit

This would be an unusual scenario. An Aquarius woman takes a long time before she commits to a relationship – and we're not just talking about marriage. Any romantic relationship will have her thinking and pondering for quite some time. She needs to get to know you. She needs to feel that you're on the same level. This is why so many Aquarians remain single for a long periods of time. If the two of you are in a relationship, it will usually mean that you have spent a long time getting to getting to know each other.

But maybe she didn't live up to your expectations. Maybe she's too independent and happy doing things on her own. If you've tried talking to her and still can't get through, it might be time to move on and seek happiness elsewhere. If she's too busy to take a hint, you may need to be a little blunt about it.

Foolproof exit measures:

Before you go ahead with any of these suggestions, be prepared to look like an idiot. She will probably get mad and tell you to get a grip before she dumps you.

- Insist on having sex frequently, passionately and on the spur of the moment
- Criticize her friends and act jealous of her male friends
- Tell her to spend more time at home
- Leave laundry and ironing for her to do
- Spend your time watching TV
- Interrupt her when she's talking and criticize her views

CHAPTER 3

SEX'N STUFF

Seductive moves:
How to get her in the mood:

Many different things turn her on, but the macho approach is not one of them. A tight t-shirt and flexed muscles won't do it for her. She needs to be aroused through imagination and anticipation. Something about her partner must be special enough to trigger her curiosity. A man with exotic, erotic knowledge will always have an advantage...

Preferences and erotic nature

An Aquarius woman gets a kick out of a creative and erotic mind. Intense passion is not that important to her. She wants to become one with her partner and experience sex on a different level. Spirituality is keyword in her sensual life. Being on the same wavelength is a must. She is turned on by the prospect of experiencing new and exciting sexual adventures – provided they are not crude or vulgar. She is also turned on by knowing that she can please her man and bring him to new erotic heights. She is an attentive lover and would never become lazy in bed. There's nothing cynical about her sex life. Everything she does is based in harmony, respect and attention.

Hitting the right buttons

Although every sign has areas on the body that are more sensitive than others, individual sensitivity may vary quite a bit. Don't go body-blind. Honing in on these erogenous zones and forgetting the rest of her is not a good idea. Use these areas to create sparks while turning her on, and as a passion-booster when things get heated. Watch her body language – including the most obvious of signs. Open your mind to the sensuality of touch and taste.

Key areas
Her calves and ankles

Get it on
Pay attention to her calves and ankles. Be creative about it, and you'll discover that there are many ways to arouse her. No matter what you do, be gentle. If your touch is too rough, you'll turn her off.

Arouse her
Practice a bit of harmless foot flirting when you're out. Use as much of your foot and leg as you can to stimulate hers. In private, there are many different ways to play with these sensitive areas. A bath will give you an opportunity to focus on her feet. Follow up with a gentle foot massage, and the erotic temperature will be rising...

Surprise her

Gentle kisses and nibbles around her ankles will make her tingle. Use a bit of honey or whipped cream to make the experience even more sensual. While kissing one leg, gently caress the other. Don't rush it. Take your time.

Spice it up

Warm oil around her ankles and a gentle massage may seem innocent, but this can spark the passion in her. The temperature will make the sensation more intense. Apply it generously and let your fingers slide gently over her ankles.

Remember: Never be blunt when trying to seduce her. Take it slow and appeal to her imagination. A slightly erotic visual – nothing graphic! – may spark her imagination.

Her expectations

Go exploring. She is a warm and exciting lover who enjoys exploring the mysteries of sex.

Let the creativity flow. You will soon discover that she is very imaginative – more than the average woman.

Try something new. Doing the same routine over and over again bores her. She will persuade her partner to try new things, or different variations of traditional positions.

Touch her gently. She enjoys caressing her partner's body, preferably when he is caressing hers at the same time.

A sassy whisper. She appreciates a man who stimulates her mind by whispering erotic words into her ear during sex. This can bring out the playfulness in her.

Playful suggestions. Her sexual philosophy is: 'What pleases him pleases me.' This means that she enjoys a wide variety of activities, provided they're not too crude or kinky.

If it's good, let her know. It's very important to her that her partner clearly expresses his enjoyment of what she's doing.

Share your fantasies. She is very open-minded and appreciates a partner who talks about his fantasies.

Your sensual preferences
Quiz yourself and find out whether this woman is for you.

Where on the scale are you?
1 = Don't agree | 3 = Sure | 5 = Agree!

1. Exploring the nuances of sex is more important than a quick climax.
One a scale for 1 to 5, you are: 1 - 2 - 3- 4 - 5

2. Communication through touch and whispers is important during sex.
One a scale for 1 to 5, you are: 1 - 2 - 3- 4 - 5

3. It's important that a woman participates actively during sex.
One a scale for 1 to 5, you are: 1 - 2 - 3- 4 - 5

4. Foreplay is important and starts before the clothes come off.
One a scale for 1 to 5, you are: 1 - 2 - 3- 4 - 5

Score.
15 - 20: This will never be boring. You both appreciate new experiences, closeness and playful pleasures ... enjoy!
10 - 14: She may take you by surprise at times, but this will only make the erotic experience more exciting.
05 - 09: Sometimes you just want to make it quick and passionate. Let her know how you feel.
01 - 04: She's either too demanding, or you are too passionate. Communication is the key to enjoyment.

CHAPTER 4

GENERAL STUFF

The big picture

Keep in mind that the characteristics of an Aquarius may vary quite a bit depending on where within the sign she was born, as well as a wide range of additional astrological factors. But for now, let's stick to the basics. Just remember: don't jump to conclusions as soon as you meet her. Give her room to shine. Get to know the woman behind the sign.

Her personality: Pros and cons

Pros	Cons
• Sparkling	• Emotionally detached
• Friendly	• Restless
• Adventurous	• Indecisive about love
• Outgoing	• Self-centred
• Kind	• A slow starter erotically
• Understanding	• Ignores her feelings
• Independent	• Naïve
• Creative	• Prone to drift
• Curious	• Indecisive
• Original	• Insecure
• Not afraid to start over	• Insensitive to other's feelings
• Enthusiastic	• Impractical
• Supportive	• Self-pitying
• An erotic explorer	• Emotionally ignorant

Tip: How to show romantic interest

Take her to a gathering or event that relates to something she is interested in. She needs to feel mentally connected with her partner, and this is a good place to start.

Romantic Vibes

Miss Aquarius:
The enthusiastic and feminine partner

The essence

The friend-zone. Everything starts with friendship, and the friendship will continue even when things get a little more intimate and romantic. The challenge is the transition from friendship to romance. If you don't manage to spark her romantic interest, you'll remain in the 'friends' zone.

Independent. She is an independent partner and doesn't mind pursuing her own interests.

Absentminded. There are always things running through her mind and may come across as a little distracted and emotionally distant sometimes. It's not her intention to withhold her feelings; she just assumes her partner knows.

No mind-reader. She may be unaware of her partner's emotional needs unless he tells her. Her emotional antennas are not particularly well tuned.

Share her energy. She is positive and sparkling and will approach a relationship with enthusiasm – provided that her partner shares her optimism. A slow and unimaginative man will drain her energy and make her feel miserable.

Quality time. She loves having people around, but she also values intimacy – both mental and sensual – with her partner.

Tip: How to show erotic interest

Be creative about it. Casually ask her about exotic sensuality, such as tantric sex, and whether it's just a fad or actually something that can increase sensual pleasure.

Erotic Vibrations

Miss Aquarius:
The adventurous and considerate lover

The essence

Gentle in her ways. There is nothing aggressive about her – she may be assertive, but never pushy.

Understanding. She takes great pride in pleasing her partner. As part of this, she is very understanding. If things are moving slowly, she will patiently arouse her partner until he is roaring to go.

Erotic explorer. Adventure is important to her, and she will explore new variations of old themes in order to keep her sex life fresh and exciting.

Sensual firework. Although she may come across as a slow mover, there's nothing slow about her. She will turn out to be a firework of sexual pleasures.

Erotic spice. When she's in the right mood, she is eager to try out different ideas. She is very imaginative and has a unique ability to brighten things up with erotic spice.

Intimacy means a lot to her. Caresses and gentle touches are paramount for her to achieve sensual pleasure.

Mutual pleasure. Pleasing her partner is just as important to her as pleasing herself – sometimes even more so. Paying close attention to her partner's needs comes naturally to her.

CHAPTER 5

COMPATIBILITY QUIZ

Are you banging your head against the wall, or does she unleash your positive potential? Do you provoke her or bring out the best in her? Is she making you throw your arms into the air in exasperation, or do you feel inspired and complete in her company? Take the test to find out.

Question 1
Have you ever toyed with the idea of trying erotic activities that are a little out of the ordinary?

A. Well, I do have fantasies, but I tend to leave them at that.
B. No, I prefer to keep it safe and comfortable!
C. Yes, several times. I have even tried tantric sex – it's very satisfying.

Question 2
During sex, your partner suddenly stops what she's doing and starts telling you about something exciting that happened to her earlier that day. Well..?

A. I guess that's my cue to sleep.
B. I would probably forget about the sex. My partner is engaging and entertaining, and I always get a kick out of listening to her.
C. Typical. I would laugh and hit her over the head with a pillow.

(cont.)

Question 3.
You wake up one morning feeling really hot. How do you react when your partner ignores you and starts telling you about her plans for the day?

A. No big deal. I can be pretty enthusiastic myself.
B. I would just pull the blanket over my head and 'sort things out' on my own.
C. My immediate reply would be: Fine, but make sure to wear something sassy when you get back...

Question 4.
Your 'toolbox' is not functioning properly one evening. What would you prefer your partner to do?

A. Focusing on herself while keeping an eye on me.
B. Nothing. Just leave me alone.
C. Show affection, play around with my tools a little bit and see what happens.

Question 5.
Would it surprise you if your partner asked you to tell her about your previous sexual experiences?

A. Not at all. Sharing sexual history is an important part of developing a healthy sex life.
B. Maybe. It would probably make me a little shy.
C. My previous sexual experiences are nobody's business.

Question 6.
Are you adaptable?

A. Not really.
B. Yes. I have a great time anywhere I go.
C. Yes, but reluctantly.

Question 7.
Does it bother you that your partner doesn't seem particularly dependent on you?

A. Not at all. In fact, it makes me feel good. I'm glad she's independent.
B. Yes. it's my biggest worry. I'm quite jealous.
C. I've got mixed feelings. I'm glad she's independent, but I want to be a part of her life, and to have a voice in her life.

Question 8.
Do you sometimes get the impression that your partner is more interested in your mind than your body?

A. Yes – and although I know I should take it as a compliment, it can make me feel a little annoyed.
B. Mind and body? They're the same thing, aren't they?
C. She likes me. That's good enough for me.

Question 9.
Have you ever got so carried away during foreplay that you forgot about an orgasm?

A. No! That's impossible.
B. Once or twice, and only when I've been in a playful mood.
C. Several times. Sex is much more than just orgasms.

Question 10.
Are you impulsive?

A. Yes, very. My friends tell me I'm a little too impulsive at times.
B. No, I firmly believe in making plans!
C. Sometimes, if I'm not busy.

SCORE	A	B	C
Question 1	5	1	10
Question 2	1	10	5
Question 3	10	5	1
Question 4	5	1	10
Question 5	10	5	1
Question 6	1	10	5
Question 7	10	1	5
Question 8	5	10	1
Question 9	1	5	10
Question 10	10	1	5

75 – 100

Do you ever find time to go out and visit your friends? Chances are that the two of you enjoy each other's company so much that you tend to get absorbed in your collective adventures, ideas and anything that can broaden your horizons. You have discovered a new energy in life, which you apply in every context– including sex. Every day holds something new for you to explore. Stick with her and you will never be bored.

51 – 74

Make sure to be open and communicative, and there won't be many bumps in the road. She is a free spirit – but this inspires you more than it bothers you. It's liberating to have a woman around who wakes up every morning and embraces the world. She makes you dream and feel alive. In return, you give her the strength and security she longs for – even if she doesn't admit it. Sensuality brings you together and allows you to connect on different levels. Nurture this relationship.

26 – 50

Are you out of breath? Slow down for a second and think. Are you attracted to the adventures, or are you attracted to the woman? She is impulsive and brings out the energy in you, but does she make you feel alive or worn out? In order to get the most out of this relationship, you need to figure out whether she satisfies your basic needs. If she doesn't, it won't last forever. If she does, it might be a good idea to communicate n order to avoid misunderstandings. Try being a bit more flexible and adaptable. This will make her feel more relaxed. And if you want to change something, tell her. She is no mind-reader.

10 – 25

Things could probably be a lot better. Why are you sticking Have you ever tried to capture a butterfly without damaging its wings? Whenever you want to discuss something important or experience a passionate moment, she is usually off somewhere on her own. This is not the basis for your perfect relationship. Although she's entertaining and interesting, there's something missing. Life feels hurried and superficial. There's never time for any depth. Unless you are on the same level, it will be difficult to make her understand and adjust. Happiness and fulfillment wait elsewhere – for both of you.

Thoughts...
It's love, not a partner quiz, that determines the future of your relationship.

...just a final note:
This book has not been approved by your date and should be treated accordingly. He or she *may* not agree with the content.